The Black Woman's Plight, Pathology & Health:
The Construction of Identity, Reality & Insanity
Individual, Couple, Professional and Family
Matters

Dear Professor:

Dissertation: The Black Woman's
Plight, Pathology & Health: The
Construction of Identity, Reality &
Insanity.
Individual, Couples, Professional
& Family Matters

As I build my paper with sections, I
wanted to build a draft of my family
origin as naked as possible. I
realize I found some mistakes. I
am thinking of the process to
include some strong themes to add
with the literature reviews and the
outline that I have constructed.
 The health of Black women will
connect with my thought process

The Black Woman's Plight, Pathology & Health:
The Construction of Identity, Reality & Insanity
Individual, Couple, Professional and Family
Matters

as a statistical number in the
system. The elements of PTSD,
trauma patient and the elements of
woman's health and pathology.
This process will be developed
with the background information of
my family tree which will be my
mother's parents and my father's
parents. My parents and the
upbringing with my step father and
his family instead of my own father.
I think this process will make some
strong claims and strong literature
reviews that will support my case
about pathology in the black
woman's health as to PTSD,
depression and other issues of
physical diseases as to cancer and
sickle cell (blood disorders).

The Black Woman's Plight, Pathology & Health:
The Construction of Identity, Reality & Insanity
Individual, Couple, Professional and Family
Matters

I am working on how to build the APA styling and editing for this report through one or two strong empirical studies that will give me case studies in return to my own personal family origins. I am going to take section by section. This first assignment on the report is the starting clusters of brainstorming how I am going to connect all these pieces together, edit it and style it with APA. This will be a challenge. The greatest challenge is the connection of my synthesis and analysis due to my own unique stand point due to my social location and background history. I will go through the motions. I am calling this process for this program, dissertation and my

The Black Woman's Plight, Pathology & Health:
The Construction of Identity, Reality & Insanity
Individual, Couple, Professional and Family
Matters

future research to woman's health as the: Black Woman's Plight: the Construction of Identity or The Black Woman's Pathology: The Construction of Reality. I am not for sure which one will be the better suitor. I would love to pull it together somehow as to the Black Woman's Plight, Pathology and Health: The Construction of Identity, Reality and Insanity. Maybe that rings a stronger phase for my dissertation, and that is a good drafting stage for all of my assignments for every class to help me knit it all together without losing direction. These are my thoughts that I wanted to journal and share with you my goals, aspirations. I am asking for any

The Black Woman's Plight, Pathology & Health:
The Construction of Identity, Reality & Insanity
Individual, Couple, Professional and Family
Matters

recommendations or examinations to assist me in my journey. Thank you so much Dr. Adkins!

P.S. Can this journal follow me throughout my program or is it class by class. Maybe I should copy and paste this somewhere else to collect my journal entries privately as well to be safe. I will go ahead and save this collection on a thumb drive. Thank you Professor.

The Poem(s)
This is the spoken words of my drafting stages for my dissertation. Eternal Work in progression and under construction.

The Black Woman's Plight, Pathology & Health:
The Construction of Identity, Reality & Insanity
Individual, Couple, Professional and Family
Matters

Uncertainty and Unseen Events: Troubling Times

by Tried by the Fire, Coach K

Troubling times is nothing more than a pebble in your shoe. Life always offers us an option. We choose that option or not. As we develop mentally, we learn that we have choices in life. Sometimes, these choices are not the outcomes we desire, but nonetheless these are options that our mind conceptualized or some may get confused by the word conceptualization, so let us use the word, create or construct a way out for us through the options we can

The Black Woman's Plight, Pathology & Health:
The Construction of Identity, Reality & Insanity
Individual, Couple, Professional and Family
Matters

perceive and trust. Life's
uncertainty and unseen events,
what is this entail? What is our
generations facing these days in
life? The access to greater
troubles, and more complicated
matters, force us to search for
solutions or run from what we think
is an only exit route or escape
plan. But, honestly, we must
search deeper and manifest new
horizons of realities through
the Phoenix ways, but how do we
awaken the Phoenix within? It is
our struggle that keep us fighting,
and exhausted, so what is the
approach to uncertainty and
unseen troubles? The fact that we
have limited resources, limited
space, restricted conclusions, our

world seem to be hard nose for the strongest and brightest, and shuffle the rest of us to the side as though we should just wait for our appointment to pass from one dimension to the next.

What keeps those without a playing field to excel and expand territories living a productive and enrich lives? The answer, what keeps us from enrich lives and empowered resources? Our ability to live from within? The treatment strategies for our existences starts with the journey of internal music. The composition of how we play melodies on our heart, mind and internal life. The music in this blog we will call therapy. It is not picking

The Black Woman's Plight, Pathology & Health:
The Construction of Identity, Reality & Insanity
Individual, Couple, Professional and Family
Matters

up a flute, saxophone or trumpet,
but how do our thoughts become
the flute, saxophone and trumpet?
It is the process of changing our
lives from within. These blogs that I
write are about internal living,
internal athleticism, internal virtue,
internal wealth and finally internal
cooking. We continue to build more
industries as to this blog segment
of internal music. How do we play
jazz and the blues from within?
This ambiance of aromatherapy
with essential oils create the mood
internally, but we have to continue
to build on our properties of
internal stewardship of our
universe from within our soul. Our
connection to lucid dreaming or
visualization constructs our

understanding on how we perceive
our daily operating life of morale
and value. It is our connection to
options and attitude of uncertainty
and unseen troubles. We know that
life come in small and large
packages, and these times, the
shifts of decay has lead me to
calculate that times are failing in
aging of how we have interacted
with our living organisms around
the globe. Therefore, we have
deteriorated at a fast past on the
level of corporate life with our
neighbors. Therefore, it is
uncertainty and unseen troubles
that pressure us to miss out
opportunities, and to set low
standards for our own life. This is
not this blog. This blog empire is

The Black Woman's Plight, Pathology & Health: The Construction of Identity, Reality & Insanity Individual, Couple, Professional and Family Matters

about setting great expectations and standards for your internal portfolio.

It is learning how to buy internal resources with your internal money--time. How do we use our time wisely. Our mind is the greatest asset beside our whole totality of our existence. We are drawn to what thoughts pass course in our minds. What do I mean by that statement? What are we doing lately with our thoughts? What dominates our time when we ponder? How do we discipline ourselves to be like ants, and store up good constructions internally. How do we start that journey? These blogs are about how do we

The Black Woman's Plight, Pathology & Health:
The Construction of Identity, Reality & Insanity
Individual, Couple, Professional and Family
Matters

live a Phoenix life during troubling
times? This is about the expression
of "Rising from our Ashes" daily
and how we endure our own
"space" of opportunity or lack
thereof in opportunity. We close
our eyes to rest, to dream some of
us, and others, not, but what we
must understand is that our minds
see infinite images, and we have to
mange and organize those images
through a process of visualization
or perception. The Phoenix Ways
is not perception, but visualization.
I bet you are wondering what is the
difference. Well, we are not talking
about the English Dictionary of the
word Visualization or Perception
but the Spirit Energy of
Visualization and Perception.

Visualization is the construction of building a case which in turn is another process that we undergo to build our "internal muscle" as to fitness and work outs. Well, visualization is that journey. The other side of the argument is perception which we are given the "ideology and picture" and we go with what is given to us. As to someone's idea of paradise, could look like roses, tulips, lilies some plants and trees, and that is perception. What we are given our whole without investigation, or building blocks to our own study of what we would like to have in our own paradise. It is fine to use it as a model as a starter point of the journey, but not the destination.

The Black Woman's Plight, Pathology & Health:
The Construction of Identity, Reality & Insanity
Individual, Couple, Professional and Family
Matters

Many people are satisfied with the basic notions of what they are given in life as a safe mode living.

I am not knocking it down, but at times, it appears to be ineffective for complicated and complex troubles that we face in present moments. It is to my own personal insight, that the Phoenix creates and that is how the we rise out our ashes. It is the framework to create for an ever changing world and environment, these times, force us to create and be steadfast in prayer and meditation. What is that theory? It is the theory to have therapies, treatments that we build from within as a carpenter building a home on a vacant lot. We have that clean slate in our mind. Some of us have to clean our slates, but nonetheless, it is that journey to build from within. Now, what we choose becomes our future journey of blogs, chats and interactions about what resources we have for the internal life. Until next time, Rise out of your Ashes--each breath we take. In the world of music, play well! Tried by the Fire

A New Day! Amen! (This piece is called a New Day)

A new day! amen! so sometimes I do this when I am lead and inspired on Sundays. in the universe, there was a special son.

a family who loved their young man God. I t was in this wonderful love, power and riches, the universe, at his disposal, it is our own mystery and myths, we wrestle with the story of the royal blood of God. It is an elite age, where all the wealthy wrestle with how to rule the people. The earth rumbled when this God child appeared in the earth, the mankind, wrestled in their mind. who is this child, without a father, we call the son of Mary. I t is still in question for 1,000 years, that a child was born, to save what world. a dying world? where is such a miracle station and location, for our eyes have not seen the change as of yet. for the world dies, and we still have no idea where these deaths leave? well this fantasy turns into a bible tale, where the first born are taken to another paradise, they leave, as this transition is abrupt, it almost feels like they have been taken by Apollo (angel who destroys.) as though there are two sides of the coins, people see two sides of the story. S ome see the recycling of all material, as particles, ashes, returning to ashes, and on the other side, we see a departure, a rapture, an unseen yet sometimes seen, a flight to ascension, yet, some still wrestle, is the mind going insane? as though when the apostles, claimed to touch his hands, this messiah, they swore, to many, 500 to be an exact, saw this so called same vision, as though, these 500 became mental ill, just by the trauma of losing a best friend to death.

Did this same vision, eat, drink and be merry, touch their lips as they drank, the blood (symbolic peace treaty with God), and touch their feet as though they were anointed for a covering we now call the everlasting treaty of peace with God and mankind. I t is still a boggling departure, to separate man from its love one. as the world violently labors in pain, the channels to birth strategies of corruption and mortality, it is a miracle that on the other side of the fence, strategies are birthed to

The Black Woman's Plight, Pathology & Health:
The Construction of Identity, Reality & Insanity
Individual, Couple, Professional and Family
Matters

bring incorruptible and immortality
to all that departs. Until, the eyes
can see and hold all the truths of
the unknown and the particles of
the universe, we make daily, the
petition of our souls that rumble for
their infinite transformation, that
treaty of peace, from their
universe, not just a planet, a star,
and an existence of mortality with
the violent ones. I t is a sure hope,
a continued progression, the faith
of the reborn. thank you for the
inspiration brother in Christ ! you
know who you are! this is what I
do...write bible fantasies of the
worlds to come, as our world
transforms from mortality into
immortality, finite into infinity...a
journey back home. (just a little

The Black Woman's Plight, Pathology & Health:
The Construction of Identity, Reality & Insanity
Individual, Couple, Professional and Family
Matters

something—free fall)

What is on your mind, heart, soul and spirit? The phoenix ways are about rebirth, creative juice, rising out of the ashes, resurrecting and building life from ground up without external resources or societal norm privileges, but the internal resources to generate wealth and power and virtue. This blog today is about living a healthy life when you are at your lowest. This chat is looking into the collection of aroma therapy, music therapy, beat therapy, writing in your own journal, creative writing therapy, breathing therapy, food therapy, chat therapy, and my list has more. It is the story of your life constructions. I remember back in 1990, I thought I was going to make my family proud by service and virtue. I learned that life in all environments, constructs as much as we construct experiences. Some people call this mother nature or others call this fate, destiny or the role we play as a performance for a grandeur audience. No matter, it is the same conclusions, I thought about in 1990, my life would be perfect. But, I realize as most artist and musicians know a huge secret in creating--we must build a masterpiece from ground up. Sometimes even with scraps, and recreate its value from worthless into priceless. This process I learned about decay over the years. It is with this very decay, trees explore the possibilities of life in its decay. We too as humans have similar processes to undergo growth through seasons of decay, or our humanity's winters. My attitude had to change. It was too narrow, and the solutions were ineffective in the 90's. I learned how to meditate and pray. The ultimate therapy that made rise out of my ashes. The Phoenix in me was born. The dove in me. I realize the stronger I grew internally, the outcomes I would endure would be worth my time. Here, in 2014, I continue learn the same lessons in life. The universe is vast, and in order for me to keep up with the growing process, to stay present, and well establish; I know my mind must renew. The options that I have explored for therapy seem to always have a foundation or skeleton of nature's finest resources. This year, I have partnered with DoTERRA to explore the possibilities of the world of aromatherapy. In conclusion, I am excited to know that earth resources internal energy and electromagnetic therapy of its vibrations and energy sent to each connected soul and spirit, give us this wonder and amazement of mystery - will we finish our race? I leave you with this one vital element for your thoughts, food of the universe, turn

The Black Woman's Plight, Pathology & Health:
The Construction of Identity, Reality & Insanity
Individual, Couple, Professional and Family
Matters

your struggle into diamonds and gold. Stay tune, and I will coach you into greatness with the Phoenix Ways! Rise out of your ashes today! ~ Tried by the Fire

This is a creative piece that motivates my audience to feel the chi, energy of life, love and beauty. The infinite and immortal force within us all and through us all.

Transforming Your Life From Within

By Tried by the Fire, Coach K

The Black Woman's Plight, Pathology & Health:
The Construction of Identity, Reality & Insanity
Individual, Couple, Professional and Family
Matters

Breathing therapy. What is breathing therapy? I have learned over the years that breathing therapy is the focus of one's breathing. The sound and the beat of the breathing. I learned how to magnify the tone of my breath through blowing up balloons. Once, I figured out how to use blowing up balloons as a formula of therapy, it was my invention and innovation to breathing exercises and breathing fitness. I learned how to transform my life using the rhythmical sounds of breathing which I used to blow up balloons to symbolize the force or chi from within. I am a visionary person, so I had to create a vision for the "forever" talked about from gurus of the power of breathing exercises. I created this image to assist me in my journey of breathing exercises. After 15 minutes of these exercises, I felt light headed. I knew it was unusual and different. I did not realize it would change my life. I was on a new path of diversity. What do I mean of diversity? I did not realize that the oxygen that would circulate my entire body through these breathing exercise would make me stronger and resilient in hard and challenge circumstances. These complex events changed my life, without mentioning the actual event. But, I knew that the breathing exercise made an exceptional diversity management strategy for my thought processes,

emotional courage and soulful
outlook which in turn gave my spirit
paradises from within. What in the
world do you think I am talking
about in this blog? I am talking
about the physical fitness we are
accustom to in every day life of
swimming, jogging, weight training
and all the wonderful exercises we
use to pump up our lives to
perform better. This small act of
fitness with the breath turned into a
chi exercise as some would call
this exercise, but I call this exercise
the new world of internal fitness. I
was an external athlete, but these
breathing exercises taught me the
internal athleticism made it the
"Spirit Giant" and what is a "Soul
Giant?" I learned how to break this

concept down into pieces for others to understand it logically. As a child make a cake, it learns how to make a cake through demonstration of one's parents or a role model who make cakes. This process of learning is "knowledge base" but without the actual performance, the child cannot make cakes to the esteem of delicious results. Over time, the development of skills, practicing good technique, the child matures in their skills, response time and overall mastery of cakes. This is the methodology of cake designing from child development into a professional. Some people do not get to learn how to make cakes as a child, so their skills are given through adult focus and self-learned actions. This process is called developing a new skill. Well, in like minded in this approach to breathing exercises, I never grew up with breathing exercises. As an adult, I learned the skill by a group of mediators, and reinvented the wheel by accident. My vocal coach told me to blow balloons to assist me in my breathing for speaking and singing. I never imagined using that same exercise to build my athleticism around breathing. I have created an internal world paradise based on breathing exercises, and I have watched miracles created through my internal approach to fitness. Now let me challenge you to take this to the next step. I have been researching about aromatherapy over the years, and finally, I have aligned myself with the DoTERRA products of essential oils, to include in my breathing exercises. My fitness agenda now include not blowing up balloons only but the inhaling of lavender and other pure essential oils. I have the physician's kit that is an excellent starter kit for the "chef or athlete" of internal fitness and profession in the "Soul and Spirit Giant" living. Until next time, Rise out of your Ashes, using the Phoenix Ways. ~Stay Tuned for more. Tried by the Fire

The Black Woman's Plight, Pathology & Health:
The Construction of Identity, Reality & Insanity
Individual, Couple, Professional and Family
Matters

I remember when I first played on my first team in eighth grade. I was so very scared. I remember almost a hundred teams later that I came to a realization that understanding team leadership is servitude at its best. I learned that whether or not you are playing on a sports team, dancing for a dance company or hired by a company, a person must understand one word, service. The service to use your skills, values and knowledge while still in progress and under construction learning, developing and growing while meshing with other personalities that you may or may not get along with at the same time. It is a juggling act!

I remember when I played my first

The Black Woman's Plight, Pathology & Health:
The Construction of Identity, Reality & Insanity
Individual, Couple, Professional and Family
Matters

sport. The try outs were daunting.
After years later, as an adult I
remember my first interview with
my first job at the high school.
Now, as an entrepreneur I
understand the concept of humble
and morale. The black belt energy
is very important. I learned this
theory in my Masters program for
Business Communications. The
text book author, Richard Schuttler
made some excellent points about
the black belt spirit. I have learned
that team building is not always
about getting the strongest,
smartest and fastest group of
people together. Sometimes it
means finding those who have
determination, heart to endure
hardship, challenge and intentions

to be interested in the mission, vision and objectives of the team.

It never fails when the world think of building a team, people think of like mindedness. Corporations set up expensive test to rate your IQ, character, credit and assess people's ability to be managed and roll with the punches. Now think about it, if the building is burning what type of people do you want on your team? It does not matter if the culture is different, disabled or blind. It matters that the job is done well and effective. At the end of the day, the question is not what is the background of the person per say, but what is the end result. Who can handle the mess? Who can handle the stress? These are the right questions when building a team.

It is a strong asset for a team to have diversity. The moment a team walked on the court, our team players always looked that team up and down looking for the weakest link. It is a sad truth, but every time have a weak point and weak moment. The question is not finding a perfect team, but finding the right team with weak points and moments that are adjustable and repairable. The question is not how to avoid conflict or mystery weaknesses by assessing people's weakness, but counting the cost of how much will it cost to repair, rehabilitate and restore if something should happen. A team should be built based on cost effectiveness to how much will it cost for the weakness of each individual. If the cost are low, or within budget then training and strategic plans for the team building will have to coach through some down time to build those skills in increments.

Last but not least, the crucial role of building a team is the rhythm and soul of the team. Yes, the black belt spirit is the grace of the team, but what is the grind in the team? What is the soul of the team? The most important part of building a team is what is the song of the team, the dance and that is the rhythm of the team. Make sure the selection of people have a sense of humor and creative. Good technique is very important in building a team, coaching and strong support structures to master weakness, but the meshing of a team is the soul. Each individual must have some percentage of attitude of humor that is tactful and real.

Note to close out for this create graffiti wall.

This work is an expression, a draft into bigger things in the near future. I am recording and publishing all documentations of all my journal entries, so I can make

The Black Woman's Plight, Pathology & Health:
The Construction of Identity, Reality & Insanity
Individual, Couple, Professional and Family
Matters

sure I have the opportunity to see the process and snow ball effectiveness to my growth and development whether professionally, academically or socially. In the Peace Treaty of God, spirituality and immortality.

Coach K